PRINCESS TEA

PRINCESS TEA

parties and treats for little girls

by Janeen A. Sarlin *with* Noelle Shipley

photographs by Sheri Giblin

CHRONICLE BOOKS
SAN FRANCISCO

dedication

To Sharon Shipley, whose tea-party dream has now materialized for our daughters and granddaughters and their granddaughters.

acknowledgments

I send my heartfelt gratitude to: Michelle and Noelle Shipley, for asking me to write this book and for sleuthing the sources. Paige Sarlin, for her encouragement, excellent writing advice, and vision. Katrina Marsh Sarlin, for her crafty ideas and fancy footwork help. Mary Lou Heiss, for her trusted tea advice and helpful suggestions. Haley and Lauren Fox, expert tea-party entrepreneurs, for wisdom beyond their years. Lisa Ekus and Jane Falla, for their professional guidance. Amy Treadwell, for always answering my queries with grace and good cheer. To Karen Liu, Kay David, Justine Noh, Emily Snider, Karen Johnson, and Edith Wilson, for offering good ideas and suggestions. Finally, thank you to the numerous grandchildren who happily taste-tested both teas and treats. *Xoxo Janeen A. Sarlin*

Library of Congress Cataloging-in-Publication Data available.
ISBN: 978-0-8118-6177-9

Manufactured in China.

DESIGNED BY Jennifer Tolo Pierce
PROP STYLING BY Ethel Brennan
PHOTOGRAPHY ASSISTANCE BY Melanie Duerkopp AND Stacy Ventura
PROP STYLING ASSISTANCE BY Melissa Coelho
FOOD STYLING BY Erin Quon
FOOD STYLING ASSISTANCE BY Viki Woolard

Thank you to stylist assistant Melissa Coelho for all her help, Patti Brunn and Fred Womack of Maison d'Etre and China McKay of Ellington and French for lending us props from their beautiful shops, and to Lynn Mumaw and Jim Hyatt for the use of their farm. And an enormous thank you to our little princesses Isabel Bevía, Charlotte Ferguson, Amina Fuller, Trai Holmes, Alexis Johnson, Zoe Keane, Elizabeth Lurssen, Suki, Mayeno, Ariella Seidman-Parra, Lola Watts, and Christen Wiley. —Sheri Giblin

10 9 8 7 6 5 4 3 2 1

Chronicle Books LLC
680 Second Street
San Francisco, California 94107

www.chroniclebooks.com

preface

Princess Tea materialized out of the vision of a book
the late Sharon Shipley wanted to write for her granddaughters
Kaitlyn and Sarah Shipley. Sharon and I had traveled throughout
Europe with her daughters, Michelle and Noelle. After her death
they asked me, their "New York Mom," to realize Sharon's dream.
In 2007, Noelle and I embarked together on a journey to create
a book to help grandmothers, mothers, and friends host magical
princess tea parties that no one will forget.

table of contents

introduction

When you and your dollies,
So festive and jolly
Sit down to your afternoon tea,
Since I can't come tripping
To join in your sipping,
Please drink a wee cupful for me.
—FROM A NINETEENTH-CENTURY GREETING CARD

Every little girl wants to be a princess. This has been true for centuries, and now that there are fewer kingdoms to rule, the desire is stronger than ever. One of the responsibilities of being a princess is entertaining courtiers and other dignitaries, and there's no better way for a princess to frolic with other princesses and parade her royal status before her subjects than at an afternoon tea party.

The current princess craze is everywhere. Walk into any store, whether high end or bargain dollar, and you will find "princess" book bags, shoes, dresses, notebooks, pencils, umbrellas, and T-shirts. This worldwide fascination is especially true of little girls from the ages of four to ten, who also happen to be prime candidates for enjoying tea parties.

Remember your first tea set? Mine was a miniature china teapot with tiny cups and saucers that I used to serve imaginary guests. I also had a small pink teapot with cups, saucers, and plates in matching shades of pale blue, pink, yellow, and green that I used for real friends. Receiving this pretty tea set was the catalyst for throwing my first tea party, with a teddy bear and my favorite doll in attendance. The scene was simple: a table, two chairs, a tea set, and my little-girl imagination, imitating my mother and grandmother.

I shared my very first cups of tea with my maternal grandmother, along with special cookies Grams made for "just us girls." Often my mother joined us, too, and we'd have three generations of women relating to each other over tea around the kitchen table. At the time, I thought everyone took breaks for afternoon tea. About thirty years later, my daughter Paige and I would drink tea after school at the living room coffee table. Sometimes we invited Mrs. Loeb, our neighbor from across the hall, but mostly it was just the two of us having tea with good conversation and a little sweet something to eat.

You can help create special memories like these for the princesses in your life, but you'll need to decide which of the eight parties in this book to try first. It probably will be a hard decision. Your choices include China, the South Sea Islands, the Southwest United States, Mexico, France, India, Africa, and, finally, a Fairy Princess Land. You don't need tickets or reservations to reach any of these faraway kingdoms, but once you decide, check for supplies you may already have on hand and note what else you'll need. Each tea party has five components: teas and juices, costumes, crafts and activities, recipes, and decorations. Remember that all of these can be customized or changed, and the themes may be seen as catalysts for the creative ingenuity of you and your princess.

Before we get started, a few basics.

TEA

Because it's usually best not to give children caffeinated teas, I have chosen herbal teas that reflect flavors found in the country or region of each party's kingdom. It is helpful to know that unlike flavored black or green teas, herbal tea packages usually list actual ingredients such as apple, mango, lemon, verbena, mint, etc. Rather than buying herbal teas simply by name, you also should consult the ingredients list on the package to find the exact taste you want for each tea party.

For each of the parties, I've suggested a couple of commercial teas, plus a juice substitute if you'd rather not serve tea. Many of these teas are readily available in markets under the brand names Bigelow, Celestial Seasonings, Republic of Tea, and Stash Tea. If you're having trouble finding the flavors you want, consult the Sources List on page 114. You can also experiment with making your own herbal infusions, and some good tea reference books are also listed in the sources section if you'd like to pursue that option.

Basic Tea-Brewing Tips

* Always start with fresh cold water.
* Use a clean teapot.
* Add tea or tea bags to the pot and pour the hot water over the tea.
* Brew tea according to directions on the package or personal preference.
* To prevent cloudiness, allow tea to come to room temperature before refrigerating.

Other than these tips, there are no hard and fast rules for brewing herbal tea. It is important to know you can't really overbrew it, so don't be overly concerned about keeping an eye on the clock.

I suggest using 1½ to 2 teaspoons (1 tea bag) of dried herbal tea for each 8 ounces of water (although most tea connoisseurs measure 6 ounces of water to a cup, we are brewing tea for little girls, who, in my experience, like slightly weaker tea). If you have fresh mint or other herbs in the garden, use 2 tablespoons of fresh leaves per cup of water. It's a good idea to make a cup of the specific tea you're planning to brew for the party ahead of time to determine the strength you like.

You can add spices such as cinnamon sticks or cardamom pods to tea for extra flavor. Just steep them for 5 to 8 minutes in boiling water, then remove and discard the spices to prevent bitterness. Next, add the tea leaves or bags and brew the tea with the flavored pot of water.

TEA TREATS

When serving a proper tea, of course one immediately thinks of treats to accompany it. I've included a wealth of recipes in this book, geared to each themed party. The classic teatime treat, though, is a tea sandwich. Traditional tea sandwiches are dainty, about two or three bites each, so they are perfect for these parties.

Basic Tea-Sandwich Instructions

* Use thinly sliced sandwich bread.

* Use a serrated knife to cut off the crusts (stack 4 slices of bread at a time).

* Line a tray with plastic wrap and place a layer of damp paper towels on top of the plastic.

* Working with 2 slices of bread at a time, cut the bread into thirds or quarters with a serrated knife, or use a cookie cutter to cut it into shapes.

* Using a butter or table knife, spread room temperature unsalted butter all the way to the edges of the bread slices.

* Add filling to half the slices, top with a slice of bread, and gently press the sandwiches together.

* Transfer the sandwiches to the prepared tray.

* Place another damp paper towel on top to prevent the sandwiches from drying out.

* Cover with plastic wrap and refrigerate until serving.

Whatever you choose to serve, remember that tea parties require fun, special party food, but that it still can be healthy. All the tea treats in this book are special because they are homemade with love and special concern for growing bodies. As a general rule, I recommend using organic products. Whenever possible, I buy vegetables and fruits from local organic farmers, and I urge you to do the same. In the recipes, I have specified organic products when I felt it would improve the outcome, but commercial ingredients will bring success as well.

Finally, remember that princesses like to participate, so get yours involved early in the party planning. If your princess also likes to cook, ask her to join you in the kitchen . . . and sip a cup of tea while the two of you work.

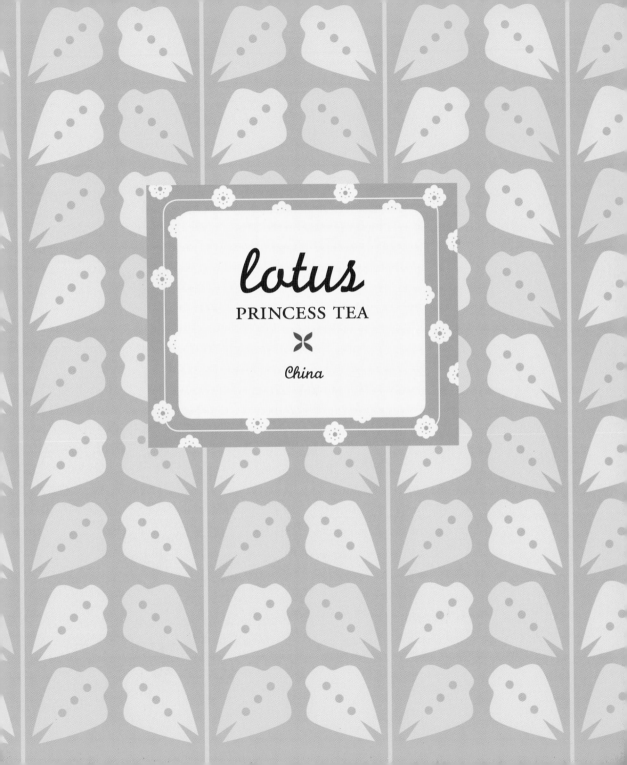

lotus

PRINCESS TEA

China

FOR THIS PARTY, GREET YOUR YOUNG ROYALTY WITH colorful yellow chrysanthemums (which symbolize hospitality), paper lanterns and dragons, wind chimes, and lute or gong music. Invite the princesses to remove their street shoes at the door and slip on bamboo flip-flops or pretty paper slippers. After settling into this exotic Asian atmosphere, the Lotus Princesses will sip lemongrass-jasmine tea from straight-sided teacups, use chopsticks to eat wontons, and create artistic designs on paper and then transform their artwork into fans.

beverage suggestions

Iced lemongrass-jasmine or hot ginger twist tea, or mandarin orange juice

costume suggestion

Colorful Mandarin-style silk blouses and slacks or kimono-style robes, and bamboo flip-flops. Lotus princesses wear their hair pulled back in ponytails and accented with flowers or chopsticks.

craft/activity

Make Paper Fans

recipes

Steamed Vegetable Wontons
Chinese Barbecue Drumsticks
Green-Tea-Ice-Cream Parasol Princesses
Apple Blossoms

decorate the space

✴

To create your exotic Asian locale, hang paper lanterns and dragons on the wall or from the ceiling, and decorate the room with pots of yellow chrysanthemums. Use bamboo placemats on the table and a lazy Susan (if you have one) in the center. Small plates, chopsticks, teacups without handles, panda bears, and fortune cookies complete the setting. You should be able to find fortune cookies in a local Asian grocery store. If not, you can order them from one of the sources listed on page 114.

make paper fans

✖

Lotus Princesses will love flirting and fanning themselves with these pretty homemade fans at the party. When the girls aren't hiding their faces behind them, the fans will dangle from their wrists.

Ten 8½-by-11-inch sheets of white or solid-color construction or rice paper (one per guest plus a few extra for mistakes)

3 sets of crayons or colored pencils (to be shared)

Samples of Chinese letter forms

8 black magic markers

4 glitter glue sticks

Paper clips

About 2½ yards red grosgrain ribbon or yarn, cut into 12- to 14-inch lengths

Nontoxic glue, or clear or red tape

Stapler

1 Instruct the princesses to draw designs on the paper. Older girls may trace or draw Chinese characters with black markers, while younger ones may draw free-form designs with the glitter glue sticks. All may embellish with crayons as desired.

2 Once the artwork is completed and dry, help the girls fold the decorated paper, beginning from the short end, into an accordion pleat. Make one fold of about ½ inch, then fold back in the opposite direction, repeating over and under about 15 times in even increments. Hold the folds together at one end and secure them with a paper clip.

3 Fold a ribbon in half to make a wrist loop. Make a knot, tying the two loose ends together and leaving about 1 to 1½ inches hanging at the end. Glue one loose end of the ribbon to the outside of the paper-clipped fan base and the other end to the other side. Then either staple, glue, or tape the fan end together, attaching the ribbon as a wrist loop as you form the handle. Each princess will be able to hang the fan on her wrist when it is not in use.

recipes

steamed vegetable wontons

MAKES 36 WONTONS

You can find wonton wrappers in the produce section of many supermarkets. They are easy to work with, and leftover wrappers can be frozen for another use. But if the thought of making wontons just seems too overwhelming, check the frozen appetizers section of your supermarket or an Asian grocery store for premade wontons.

VEGETABLE FILLING

2 carrots, peeled and thinly shredded

1 stalk celery, peeled and
finely chopped

2 medium zucchini, finely chopped

12 snow peas, strings removed
and cut into thin slivers

4 to 6 scallions, finely chopped

1 clove garlic, minced

3 water chestnuts, drained
and finely diced

½ teaspoon sugar

1 tablespoon soy sauce

½ teaspoon sesame oil

About 1 tablespoon oyster sauce

1 To prepare the vegetable filling: In a large mixing bowl, toss the vegetables, garlic, and water chestnuts together. In a small bowl, mix together the sugar, soy sauce, sesame oil, oyster sauce, cornstarch, and egg together. Stir this mixture into the vegetables until well blended. To taste and adjust the seasonings, cook or steam 1 tablespoon of the mixture in a small skillet over low heat, or in the microwave for thirty seconds.

2 To assemble the wontons: Take the wonton wrappers out of the refrigerator and put a small bowl of water on the work surface. Remove the plastic wrap and the paper coating the wonton wrappers. As you use them, keep the wrappers covered with a damp paper towel to prevent them from drying out.

continued . . .

1½ tablespoons cornstarch

1 egg, beaten

WONTONS

36 wonton wrappers

10 cups cold water

1 tablespoon salt

1 tablespoon peanut oil

Soy sauce for dipping

3 Place 1 tablespoon of the filling in the center of the unfloured side of a wonton wrapper (one side of each wrapper is floured). Dip your finger into the water and wet all the edges of the wrapper. Fold one side of the wrapper over the filling, pulling it to the opposite edge and sealing it like an envelope. Then wet the two corners and pinch them together to form a wonton. (The first one you make may seem awkward, but after you make two or three it's fun!) As you make them, place the wontons on a baking sheet (floured to prevent sticking) until all the wontons are ready to cook.

4 Fill a large pot with the 10 cups of water and add the salt and peanut oil. Bring the water to a boil over high heat. Use a wire-mesh skimmer/ strainer to add the wontons to the pot, about 6 at a time, to prevent them from sticking to each other. Cook until all of the wrappers are translucent, 7 to 8 minutes. Drain the wontons in a colander, shaking off excess water. Transfer the cooked wontons to a baking sheet and let them cool for about 5 minutes before serving. Or cool completely, store in plastic bags, and refrigerate. Just before serving, remove wontons from the bags and reheat them in a steamer basket over simmering water, about 1 minute. Serve with the soy sauce.

chinese barbecue drumsticks

MAKES 6 SERVINGS

Most little girls like carrot sticks. Using them to form the outline of a drum on their plate adds to the festivities. These sticky drumsticks are finger food, so be sure to pass out warm wet washcloths or moist towelettes for cleanup.

8 tablespoons ketchup

4 tablespoons clover blossom honey

2 tablespoons rice wine vinegar

2 tablespoons soy sauce

2 small cloves garlic, minced

12 small chicken drumsticks, washed and patted dry

3 medium carrots, peeled and cut into thin 2-inch sticks

1 In a small mixing bowl, whisk together the ketchup, honey, vinegar, soy sauce, and garlic. Mix well and taste, and adjust for balance of flavors. Place the drumsticks in a large bowl or zip-top bag and cover with the sauce to coat. Cover or seal and refrigerate for about 30 minutes or up to 2 hours.

2 Preheat the oven to 350°F. Choose a baking pan large enough to hold all the drumsticks in one layer and line it with parchment paper. Arrange the drumsticks in the pan and bake until the juices run clear when pierced with a fork, turning two or three times to ensure even browning, 30 to 40 minutes. Remove from the oven and let stand for at least 10 minutes before serving.

3 To serve, arrange carrot sticks to form a drum on each plate, and place drumsticks on top.

green·tea·ice·cream parasol princesses

MAKES 6 SERVINGS

Festive tiny paper parasols, which you can find at many supermarkets and novelty stores, complete the look of these adorable ice-cream princesses. For best presentation, use small tea or demitasse saucers to serve the ice cream.

2 pints green tea ice cream

1 bag black licorice ropes

1 jar maraschino cherries, drained

6 small paper parasols

1 With a round ice-cream scoop, dip 6 smooth scoops of the ice cream. Set them on a plastic wrap–lined tray that can accommodate them in one layer.

2 Decorate the scoops with licorice and cherries to make the faces of the princesses. Use snippets of licorice for the eyes and nose, and ¼ cherry for the lips. Make 6 small coils of licorice for hair and place one coil on top of each of the ice-cream faces.

3 Put the tray of ice cream in the freezer and freeze until solid. Wrap each face in plastic wrap and place in a plastic container to protect them. Store in the freezer for up to 1 day before the party.

4 To serve, unwrap the ice-cream faces, set them on small flat saucers, and place an opened parasol behind each one.

apple blossoms

You can offer healthful options such as dried blueberries, cherries, or sunflower seeds to substitute for or add to the raisins in this recipe, so each princess can create her flower according to her own liking. Most kids like red or yellow crisp, crunchy apples rather than soft, mealy ones. For even more festive decorating possibilities, look for multicolored marshmallows in the organic section of the market.

6 small-to-medium Pink Lady or Red Delicious apples

1 lemon, cut in half

6 large marshmallows, plus extra for snacking, preferably organic

½ cup raisins, plus extra for snacking

1 Cut each apple into quarters and remove the core. Cut each quarter in half to make 8 flower petals. Rub both sides of each apple slice with the cut side of the lemon, to prevent discoloration. Arrange the apple slices on separate plates like the petals of a flower.

2 Using kitchen scissors, cut just the top of each marshmallow into quarters, leaving the base uncut. Fill the center of the marshmallows with raisins, and place one in the center of each of the apple flowers. Set out bowls of extra marshmallows and raisins for snacking.

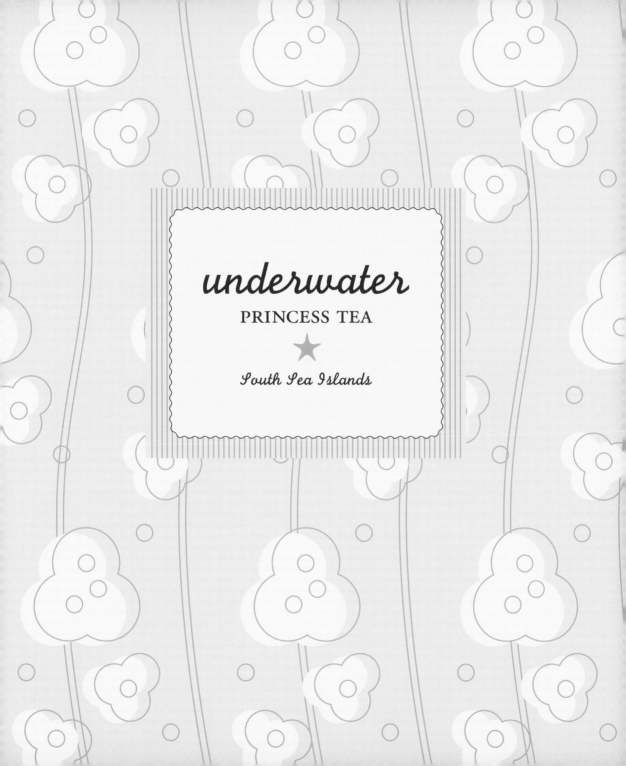

underwater

PRINCESS TEA

★

South Sea Islands

IF YOU HAVE A SWIMMING POOL,
you probably already have all the props you need for this setting.
Be sure to have a lifeguard on duty, and supply floats, flippers,
goggles, and a big stack of beach towels. No pool? Not a problem.
Create a nautical feeling with real or blow-up fish, fishnets, lobster
traps, sand pails, and sailboats. The young mermaids will feast on
fishy tuna sandwiches, pasta shells, and melon boats, and banana
dolphins will rise to the surface in their glasses!

beverage suggestions
Mint or hibiscus lemon tea
Limeade with Banana Dolphins

★

costume suggestion
Colorful bathing suits wrapped with a pareo or sarong, and flip-flops.
Underwater princesses wear their hair tied back (or in bathing caps if there's a pool).
Alternatively, you could create mermaid costumes.

★

craft/activity
Make Finger Paintings

★

recipes
Cucumber Crocodile Centerpiece
Fishy Tuna Tea Sandwiches
Buttered Seashells with Goldfish
Seashore Sand Cookies
Melon Sailboats

decorate the space

★

To create your undersea kingdom, cover the table with aqua-colored fabric or a seashell-patterned tablecloth. If you have a mirror, place the Cucumber Crocodile Centerpiece (page 29) on it in the middle of the table. Put various colors and sizes of plastic or paper fish and boat flags around the room, and fill a treasure chest with small net bags of faux jewels. Fill a glass fishbowl with goldfish crackers and another with candy Swedish fish.

  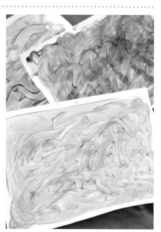

make finger paintings

★

Mermaids and swimmers become landlubber artists as they create creatures-from-the-sea finger paintings. Allow the girls to have fun creating their very own idea of an underwater wonderland. You'll need a washable table or work area for the girls to use, and a sink nearby for cleanup.

2 boxes (set of four colors) washable finger paints

Finger painting paper sheets or tablet

6 pens

1 Give each princess a space to create her painting. Encourage the girls to choose a background color for their underwater setting (blue or green are standard choices, but maybe their kingdom has a pink sea). Offer different color choices to draw fish, octopuses, crabs, etc.

2 To create an octopus with finger paint, use the inside of the palm of a hand to make the body and fingers to make the tentacles. To make a crab, place one hand directly on the paper with fingers facing to one side. Then place the other hand directly on top of the print with fingers facing the other direction. The palms make the body, the fingers create the many legs, and the thumbs represent the eyes of the crab.

3 To make a school of little fish, use fingerprints or thumbprints spaced closely together. Use a pen to draw eyes and fins on the little fish.

recipes

limeade *with* banana dolphins

MAKES 2 QUARTS

Prepare the banana dolphins ahead of time, and roll them in lime juice to prevent discoloration.

LIMEADE

1 cup fresh lime juice

About ½ cup sugar

8 cups cold water

BANANA DOLPHINS

3 medium or 6 small bananas

12 raisins

fresh lime juice

1 To prepare the limeade: Put the lime juice and sugar together in a large pitcher, and stir until the sugar is dissolved. Whisk the cold water into the juice until blended. Taste and adjust the sweetness. Refrigerate until serving time.

2 To make the banana dolphins: Peel the bananas, and cut a thin wedge out of one end of each with a small paring knife to create smiling mouths. Use 2 raisins on each to create eyes. Roll the bananas in lime juice. Stand them in glasses with the bottoms of the mouths on the rims, as if they were jumping out of the glasses. Pour in cold limeade and serve.

cucumber crocodile centerpiece

Plan to make this crocodile no sooner than about an hour before the party, to keep it looking fresh. (The carrots, green bell pepper, and radish may be prepped a little earlier.) Princesses will delight when they see this friendly crocodile—it's one they can eat, instead of the crocodile eating them!

7 or 8 carrots, peeled

About 2 tablespoons vinaigrette salad dressing

1 long English or seedless cucumber

½ red bell pepper, seeded, deribbed, and cut into a small triangle

1 green bell pepper, seeded, deribbed, and cut into 2 tiny squares and 4 small tulip shapes

1 radish, cut into slices

1 Shred the carrots into a bowl and toss with the vinaigrette. Arrange the carrots on a mirror or platter as an island or sandbar for the crocodile.

2 Cut very thin slices ¾ of the way through the cucumber along its length, to resemble the skin of a crocodile, leaving 2 inches on one end for the head. For the head, cut a diagonal slice off the top of the unsliced end to create a face; place the slice at the opposite end of the cucumber to form a tail. Then make a thin curving cut where the mouth should be, cutting out enough of the cucumber to allow space to insert the red bell pepper triangle (the crocodile's tongue). Secure the tongue with a small piece of toothpick. To make the eyes, place a tiny square of green bell pepper in the center of each of two radish slices and secure them in place with small pieces of toothpick.

3 Carefully set the crocodile on the shredded carrot island. To make the feet, place two of the tulip-shaped green bell pepper pieces on each side of the crocodile, close to the body.

fishy tuna tea sandwiches

MAKES 6 SANDWICHES

If you don't have a fish-shaped cookie cutter to cut these sandwiches into per-fect fish shapes, it's easy to make a pattern. Draw the outline of a 3- or 4-inch-long goldfish on a piece of tagboard and cut it out. Place the paper template on the center of the bread, and with a sharp paring knife follow the outline of the paper to cut out the fish. (If you use a pattern rather than a cookie cutter, it may work better to serve open-faced sandwiches.) Make the filling a day before the party and refrigerate it. The morning of the party, assemble the sandwiches and refrigerate until serving time.

Two 10-ounce cans olive oil–packed tuna fish, drained

1 to 2 teaspoons freshly squeezed lemon juice

2 to 3 scallions, minced

Sea salt

Freshly ground black pepper

1 tablespoon sweet pickle relish, drained (optional)

2 to 3 tablespoons mayonnaise

12 thin slices whole-wheat bread

About 2 tablespoons unsalted butter, at room temperature

2 to 3 pimiento-stuffed olives, cut into thin slices

1 With a fork, break up the chunks of tuna into a medium mixing bowl. Season to taste with lemon juice; add the scallions, a pinch of salt, a grinding of pepper, and the pickle relish (if using). Stir in just enough mayonnaise to bind the mixture together. Taste and adjust the seasonings. Cover and refrigerate.

2 Using a cookie cutter or pattern, cut the bread into fish shapes. Butter each of the fish, spreading the butter out to the edge of the bread. Spread an even layer of tuna salad out to the edges of half of the fish, cover with another fish, and gently press the sandwiches together. Cover with a damp paper towel, wrap in plastic wrap, and refrigerate until serving time. Just before serving, position an olive slice on each of the fish to resemble an eye, and arrange on a platter.

buttered seashells *with* goldfish

Before cooking the pasta for this recipe, cut the cheese into goldfish shapes so you can place them on top to swim over the Parmesan-dusted shells. All kids love pasta—and cheese; be sure to have plenty of Parmesan on hand.

1½ pounds shell-shaped pasta

3 to 4 tablespoons unsalted butter or olive oil

Sea salt

Freshly ground black pepper

1 cup freshly grated Parmesan cheese

¼ cup minced flat-leaf (Italian) parsley

6 slices yellow Cheddar or American cheese, cut into goldfish shapes

1 Bring a large pot of salted water to boil over high heat. Add the pasta a handful at a time, and cook according to package directions or until al dente, about 12 minutes.

2 Drain and return the pasta shells to the pot and set it back on the stove. Dot the shells with butter, season with salt and pepper, and toss well.

3 To serve, spoon the shells into individual soup or pasta bowls and sprinkle with Parmesan cheese (to resemble sand) and parsley (for seaweed), and add a cheese fish swimming on top.

seashore sand cookies

You can find 1½- to 2-inch shell-shaped metal molds in baking or cookware stores. Ground almonds give these rich cookies a granular, sandy texture. To save time, bake the cookies up to 2 weeks ahead and store them in an airtight container.

½ cup blanched almonds, roasted and salted

¾ cup (1½ sticks) unsalted butter, at room temperature

¾ cup sugar

2 teaspoons pure alcohol-free almond extract

1 egg white

2 cups flour

Pinch of fine sea salt

¼ teaspoon ground cinnamon

1 Preheat the oven to 350°F. Process the almonds until finely ground in a food processor. Add the butter, sugar, almond extract, and egg white. Process a few pulses to mix. Add the flour, salt, and cinnamon and process until blended but still "sandy." Roll the dough into balls of about 1 teaspoon each.

2 Generously grease shell-shaped metal molds with vegetable oil or solid vegetable shortening.

3 Working in batches, place the balls into the molds and press the dough into the bottoms and up the sides of the molds. Set the molds on a jelly-roll pan and bake until the dough is firm to the touch and the edges are light brown, 10 to 12 minutes. Turn off the oven and leave the cookies in for 5 minutes longer. Remove from the oven and set the molds on a wire rack, and let cool completely. Run the tip of a small knife around the edges of the molds and tap the cookies out. Store in an airtight container for up to 1 month.

melon sailboats

When choosing a cantaloupe, look for one with an unblemished rind, a slight melon aroma, and a stem end that gives a little when you press it with your thumb. For food safety, be sure to wash the rind of the melon with soap and water, rinse well, and pat dry with paper towels before cutting. Colorful flags on toothpicks form the sails for these amusing boats.

1 large ripe cantaloupe

About 25 little paper flags on toothpicks, or fresh mint leaves skewered on toothpicks to resemble flags

1 large bunch of seedless green grapes, washed and stems removed

1　Starting at the stem end, cut the cantaloupe in half and scoop out the seeds. Cut each half into quarters and each quarter into 1-inch-thick wedges that resemble boats. Make about 5 vertical cuts in each wedge, and then one long slice underneath to form little edible cabins that are easy to remove with a toothpick.

2　Place a toothpick flag at the end of each boat and arrange all the melon boats on a platter.

3　Place green seedless grapes around the edges to resemble the sea.

cowgirl

PRINCESS TEA

Southwest United States

A PICNIC TABLE ON THE PATIO OR UNDER A TREE
in the backyard is the perfect setting for this party. If space and conditions allow, add bales of straw and buckets of sunflowers and play country-and-western music in the background. The princesses will believe they have come to a Western dude ranch complete with split-rail fences, grazing cattle, and horses. After eating lip-smackin' finger foods and drinking iced tea or pink grapefruit juice, the girls will learn to line dance and paint wagon-wheel cookies with icing (allowing for individual artistic expression and interpretation). An extra bonus of frontier-style living: No silverware is required for this fun-lovin' tea party!

beverage suggestions
Iced rooibos or orange mango tea, or pink grapefruit juice

costume suggestion
Flannel or Western shirts, vests, and jeans with silver-buckled belts. Cowgirls wear their hair in pigtails, and Western boots and hats complete their outfits.

craft/activity
Paint Wagon Wheels (Cookies)
Learn a Line Dance

recipes
BBQ Cups
Finger-Lickin' Chicken Batons
Cowgirl Chocolate Chip Wagon Wheels
Crispy, Crunchy Boots

decorate the space

★

To establish the atmosphere, cover the table with Western bandanas or check-ered fabric and use kerchiefs for napkins. Add festive bouquets of fresh or paper bluebonnets or sunflowers, and pass out cowgirl hats. Knot red licorice ropes to resemble lariats, and lay them on the table.

paint wagon wheels (cookies)

★

Using a pastry bag (for 7- to 10-year-olds) or paintbrush (for 4- to 6-year-olds), the girls will draw the hubs and spokes of wagon wheels on chocolate cookies. Set out bowls of icing, and allow for unique artistic expression. Have plenty of wet washcloths or paper towels on hand for easy cleanup.

12 (or 2 per princess) undecorated Cowgirl Chocolate Chip Wagon Wheels (page 43)

1 dozen predecorated cookies, as examples

6 to 8 small plastic sandwich or pastry bags, filled with white icing (page 45)

8 new small watercolor brushes, washed

Colored sprinkles for decorating

Cooling rack

1 Lay out the undecorated and the inspiration cookies on a clean work surface.

2 Spoon some of the icing into the sandwich bags, twist the tops shut, and snip off a tiny corner of each bag to form a writing tip.

3 Show the princesses how to draw a solid circle (hub) in the center and 6 or 8 lines from the hub to the edges of the cookie to resemble the spokes of a wagon wheel.

4 Fill a few custard cups with some of the remaining icing, thinning it to the consistency of tempera paint, and let younger girls use a paintbrush to paint on the wheels. Encourage all the girls to use the sprinkles for artistic expression. Set decorated wheels on a wire rack, and let the icing set for at least 10 to 15 minutes before serving.

learn a line dance
★

Put on a country line-dance song such as "Achy Breaky Heart." Begin the dance with the princesses standing in a line. Start the music and make sure you stand in the center of the line so everyone can see the steps. Call out the following steps until the girls catch on.

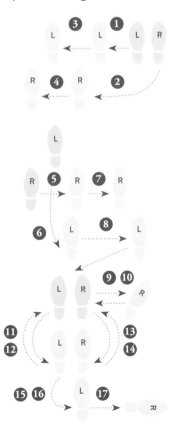

Grapevine left:
1 2 Step left foot to left, step right foot to left behind left leg.
3 4 Step left foot to left, kick right foot behind left leg, slapping heel of boot with left hand.

Grapevine right:
5 6 Step right foot to right, step left foot to right behind right leg.
7 8 Step right foot to right, kick left foot behind right leg, slapping heel of boot with right hand, step on left foot.
9 10 Touch right heel out, step right foot back to center.
11 12 Touch left toe behind right foot, bring left foot back to center.
13 14 Touch right toe behind left foot, bring right foot back to center.
15 16 Cross left foot behind right, putting weight on left foot.
17 Turn ¼ turn to right, putting weight down on right foot.

Repeat from the top.

bbq cups

MAKES 12 CUPS OR 24 MINI CUPS

My children used to beg me to make these little cups filled with barbecued beef for tea after school. The recipe is adapted from their grandmother's circa 1970 recipe collection. Make the filling the day before the party, then all that's left to do is to fill the muffin tins and bake them.

1 pound lean ground beef, preferably chuck

2 tablespoons minced onion

2 tablespoons light brown sugar

About ½ cup smoked barbecue sauce

1 can refrigerated prepared crescent rolls or biscuits

¾ cup shredded mild Cheddar cheese

1 Preheat the oven to 400°F. Lightly grease muffin tins with oil.

2 In a large skillet over high heat, cook the beef, stirring often, until browned, about 6 minutes. Add the onion and sauté until soft and translucent, about 5 minutes. Stir the sugar into the barbecue sauce and add to the beef and onion. Reduce the heat and simmer for 8 minutes. Taste and adjust the seasonings, and add more sauce if desired. Let cool.

3 Separate the dough pieces and place one in the bottom of each muffin tin, pressing the dough up the sides to form a cup. Spoon the meat mixture into each cup. Bake until the edges of the cups are golden brown, 10 to 15 minutes. Remove from the oven and top with a pinch of cheese. Return to the oven and bake until the cheese melts, about 2 minutes longer. Cool 5 to 6 minutes before serving.

finger-lickin' chicken batons

MAKES 6 SERVINGS (5 to 6 batons per princess)

Parmesan cheese and breadcrumbs keep these chicken batons moist. They are as easy as one-two-three. Be sure to have plenty of napkins on hand for finger cleanup.

4 boneless skinless chicken breasts, 7 to 8 ounces each

1 cup (2 sticks) unsalted butter, melted

1 cup grated Parmesan cheese

2 to 2½ cups seasoned fine breadcrumbs

1 Preheat the oven to 400°F. Line a jelly-roll pan with parchment paper or aluminum foil and coat it with vegetable oil.

2 Wash the chicken breasts and pat dry with paper towels. Cut the chicken into slices (batons) 2½ to 3 inches long by ½ inch wide.

3 Pour the melted butter into a shallow bowl. In another shallow bowl, mix the cheese and breadcrumbs together. Roll the chicken batons in the butter and then in the breadcrumb mixture until they are coated. Transfer them to the prepared baking pan.

4 Bake until the juices run clear when the chicken is poked with a fork and the bread-crumbs are brown, 20 to 25 minutes (baking time may vary depending on the size of the chicken batons). Arrange on a platter and let cool for about 5 minutes before serving.

cowgirl chocolate chip wagon wheels

MAKES ABOUT 6 DOZEN COOKIES

Make this cookie dough and refrigerate it a few days before the party. A day or two later, bake the cookies and store them in an airtight container (there will be extra for the family). The recipe calls for plenty of icing, just in case the cowgirls do more tasting than decorating!

COOKIES

2 squares (2 ounces) unsweetened chocolate

1 cup (2 sticks) unsalted butter at room temperature

½ cup granulated sugar

½ cup light brown sugar

2 eggs

1 tablespoon pure alcohol-free vanilla extract

2 teaspoons cinnamon

2½ cups flour

¼ cup old-fashioned oatmeal

½ teaspoon baking soda

1 teaspoon salt

½ cup chocolate chips

1½ cups chocolate sprinkles

continued . . .

1. Melt the chocolate in a small bowl set over a pan of simmering water, or microwave for 1 to 1½ minutes, and set aside to cool.

2. In a large mixing bowl, cream the butter until smooth, add the granulated and brown sugars, and beat until light and fluffy. Add the cooled chocolate and blend until there are no streaks. Add the eggs, one at a time, beating well after each addition. Add the vanilla and cinnamon.

3. In a separate bowl, mix the flour, oatmeal, baking soda, and salt together and stir into the butter mixture until blended. Stir in the chocolate chips.

4. Place waxed or parchment paper on a countertop and spoon the dough onto the paper. Using a rubber scraper or damp hands, form the dough into a long, smooth roll about 2½ inches in diameter, using the paper to shape it. Press the sprinkles into the dough, covering the outside of the roll.

ICING

1 pound (16 ounces)
confectioners' sugar

Pinch of salt

1 teaspoon pure alcohol-free
vanilla extract

4 to 6 tablespoons milk or
heavy cream

Extra sprinkles for decorating

5 Wrap the dough in another sheet of paper and then in plastic wrap, twisting the ends shut, and refrigerate until firm, up to 3 days, or freeze for up to 1 month.

6 Preheat the oven to 400°F. Remove the plastic and unroll the paper, and cut the dough into even ⅜-inch-thick slices. Place them about 1 inch apart on ungreased baking sheets. Bake until the cookies are slightly firm to the touch, about 8 minutes. Transfer to a wire rack and let cool before the party.

7 To make the icing: In a small bowl, whisk the confectioners' sugar, salt, vanilla, and just enough milk to make a medium-thick consistency icing. Fill pastry bags and decorate the cookies.

crispy, crunchy boots

MAKES ABOUT 24 BOOTS

Texas-grown pistachios add flavor and crunch to this all-time-favorite rice cereal bar. Be sure to generously "polish" the 3- to 4-inch boot cookie cutter with butter and cut out the boots before they are completely cold. Store the boots in an airtight container or wrap each one in plastic wrap.

1 bag plain marshmallows, organic if possible

¼ cup unsalted butter, cut into pieces, plus extra for greasing the pan

½ cup 2% or whole milk

2 teaspoons pure alcohol-free vanilla extract

6 cups crispy brown rice cereal, or your favorite brand

½ cup chopped salted roasted pistachios

1 Generously grease a jelly-roll pan with butter.

2 In a large metal bowl set over a pan of simmering water, mix the marshmallows, ¼ cup butter, and milk together, whisking as the marshmallows begin to melt. Whisk in the vanilla and mix well. Remove from the heat and stir in the cereal and pistachios.

3 Transfer the mixture to the prepared jelly-roll pan and with buttered hands press the mixture into the pan, spreading it into an even layer. Refrigerate for a few minutes until firm but not hard and, with a buttered cutter, cut out the cowgirl boots. Let them sit until firm.

fiesta

PRINCESS TEA

Mexico

TO CREATE A SOUTH-OF-THE-BORDER FEELING,
think warm colors, sunny days, and wonderfully rhythmic Spanish
music. The central attraction of this tea festival is a piñata for the
children to break open with sticks. A serape, a colorful striped woolen
shawl usually worn over men's shoulders, makes an ideal tablecloth,
but any vibrant fabric will work. Princesses look festive in fiesta skirts
with off-the-shoulder blouses. The food is uncomplicated to create,
so turn up the music and let the fiesta begin.

beverage suggestions
Apple-mango tea
Mexican Hot Chocolate
Watermelon Juice

✦

costume suggestion
White off-the-shoulder blouses, fiesta skirts, belts, and sombreros

✦

craft/activity
Learn the Mexican Hat Dance
Break the Piñata

✦

recipes
Guacamole
Black Bean and Monterey Jack Cheese Rolls
Fiesta Flower-Girl Cookies
Mexican Princess Cinnamon Tea Cakes

decorate the space

✿

To create a festive fiesta mood, cover the table with a serape or red tablecloth and a sombrero. Set a piñata in the center (to be broken open later) and surround it with bowls of corn chips and salsa.

learn the mexican hat dance

Begin the dance with the princesses standing in a circle around a Mexican sombrero on the floor. Put on a version of "Mexican Hat Dance," and clap to the rhythm for a few counts to get started, then teach the princesses these steps.

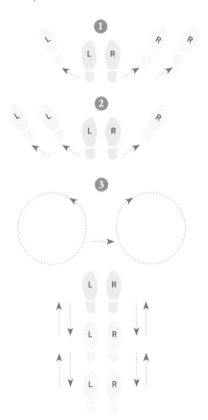

Basic foot movement:

1 Right heel front, left heel front, right heel front, clap clap.

2 Repeat to the left—a left and a right and a left, clap clap.

Rhythm: a basic four/four count: a one and a two and a three, clap clap (on four)

3 Begin by standing in place, and as the music starts, perform the basic heel-heel-clap-clap movement twice until the musical phrase changes (about thirty bars). When the music changes, have the girls skip to the left in a counterclockwise circle while holding hands. At the next music change, tell them to skip in the other direction. When the music returns to the first phrase, have the princesses stand and repeat the heel-heel-clap-clap routine. When the musical phrase changes the final time, have the girls hold hands and take two steps forward, raising their hands above their heads, then two steps back to the original circle, letting go as they swing their hands down. When the music stops, each girl twirls around once and shouts "olé!"

break the piñata

1 Hang a piñata on a tree in the yard, or from the ceiling in a porch or family room, with plenty of space around it for the princesses to swing a stick or plastic baseball bat.

2 Blindfold one princess at a time, turn her around a few times (to disorient her), hand her a stick or plastic bat, and place her in front of the piñata. Each girl gets three swings to try to break open the piñata before the next princess takes a turn. For safety reasons, two or three adults should assist in this game; please make sure everyone is out of the swing range. Once the piñata has been broken open, watch the princesses scramble for the trinkets.

mexican hot chocolate

MAKES GENEROUS 6 CUPS

Traditional Mexican hot chocolate is made with hot milk, unsweetened Mexican chocolate, cinnamon, and eggs. A *molinillo,* or carved wooden whisk, is used to bring out the "spirit" of the drink—the foam on top is believed to be evidence that the spirit is present. This simple version is easy to create with or without a *molinillo.* Be sure to let it cool for a few minutes before serving.

11 ounces chopped
semisweet chocolate
(preferably 70% cocoa solids)

1 cup boiling water

1/3 cup sugar

1½ teaspoons pure
alcohol-free vanilla extract

6 cups 2% or whole milk

Freshly grated cinnamon

6 cinnamon sticks

1 Chop or grate the chocolate onto a sheet of waxed paper. Pour the boiling water into a medium bowl and with a small whisk, stir in the chopped chocolate and sugar, whisking until it is melted and completely smooth. Whisk in the vanilla and set aside.

2 In a large saucepan over low heat, warm the milk to almost scalding and remove from the heat. With a *molinillo* or wire whisk, slowly whisk the melted chocolate mixture into the hot milk until blended and foamy. Pour into mugs, sprinkle with cinnamon, and place a cinnamon stick in each mug of hot chocolate. Let cool for a few minutes before serving.

watermelon juice

MAKES ABOUT 3 QUARTS

Only two things are needed to make this juice—a cold watermelon and a blender or food processor. The pretty pink juice tastes as refreshing as it looks. If puréeing the juice before the party, refrigerate it until the girls arrive and stir well before serving.

1 large watermelon

1 Refrigerate the watermelon overnight.

2 Wash the rind of the melon, then slice it and cut each slice into quarters. With a fork in one hand and a melon slice in the other, hold your hands over a bowl and remove all the seeds. Set a strainer over another bowl and pour the seeds and accumulated juice into the strainer. Reserve the juice and discard the seeds and the rind. Cut the watermelon into chunks and purée in a blender or processor along with the reserved juice. Pour into a pitcher and serve.

guacamole

Red bell pepper adds color and crunch to this guacamole. Mound the guacamole on a lettuce-lined platter and surround it with bowls of black olives, cilantro, and corn chips. Watch it disappear!

2 ripe large avocados,
preferably Hass

1 to 2 limes, freshly squeezed

½ medium sweet onion,
finely chopped

2 ripe tomatoes, finely chopped

½ large red bell pepper,
finely chopped

½ teaspoon sea salt

Freshly ground black pepper

1 jalapeño pepper, seeded
and minced (optional)

One 6-ounce can pitted black
olives, drained and chopped

1 bunch cilantro,
stemmed and chopped

2 bags corn chips, one blue and
one white, preferably organic

1 Cut the avocados in half, remove the pits, and scoop the flesh into a medium mixing bowl. With the side of a fork or a potato masher, mash the flesh until chunky. Add the lime juice, onion, tomatoes, bell pepper, salt, a grinding of pepper, and jalapeño (if using) and combine well. Squeeze lime juice over the guacamole to inhibit discoloration, press plastic wrap directly on top, and refrigerate until serving time.

2 To serve, mound the guacamole in a colorful bowl and accompany with the black olives, cilantro, and corn chips.

black bean and monterey jack cheese rolls

MAKES 6 ROLLS

Sprouted-wheat tortillas are a little sweeter than regular flour or corn tortillas, so kids love them. Using canned black beans is a good timesaving step. Add a few red pepper flakes and more chiles to the beans if your princesses like spicy food.

2 cups dried black beans
(or two 15-ounce cans black beans)

About 4 cups vegetable stock
or water

½ medium onion, chopped

2 cloves garlic, minced

1 ancho chile, cut in half
and seeded (optional)

Sea salt

Freshly ground black pepper

6 soft sprouted-wheat tortillas
(available at health food stores or in
the organic section of supermarkets)

About 1½ cups prepared
tomato sauce

8 ounces mild Cheddar or
Monterey Jack cheese, shredded

1 Sort and rinse the dried beans, cover with at least 4 inches of cold water, and let soak overnight.

2 Drain the water and transfer the beans to a heavy saucepan. Cover the beans with vegetable stock or fresh cold water and add the onion, garlic, and chile (if using). Cover the pan and bring to a boil over high heat. Reduce the heat and simmer until the beans are tender and easily mashed between thumb and finger. Drain the beans and transfer to a medium mixing bowl. Season with salt and pepper.

If using canned beans, simply rinse, drain, and heat them through; season as needed.

3 Spread an even layer of warm beans on the tortillas, drizzle with a spoonful of tomato sauce, and scatter the cheese on top. Starting from one side, roll the tortillas tightly and arrange them seam-side down on a plate. Like the Guacamole (page 55), these rolls are finger food.

fiesta flower-girl cookies

MAKES 48 COOKIES

It is customary at Mexican weddings to serve these rich little round cookies dusted with confectioners' sugar. They are believed to bring good luck to a couple. For the lucky girls at this party, you can roll the fiesta flower cookies in brightly colored sugar instead of confectioners' sugar. You can make the cookies ahead of time and store them in an airtight container for up to 1 week.

1 cup (2 sticks) unsalted butter, at room temperature

½ cup confectioners' sugar

1 tablespoons pure alcohol-free vanilla extract

2¼ cups flour

¼ teaspoon salt

¾ cup finely chopped toasted pecans

About 1½ cups colored sugar, mixed (red, orange, yellow, and green)

1 In a medium bowl, using an electric mixer, cream the butter and sugar together until light and fluffy, and add the vanilla. Stir in the flour and salt and blend. Mix in the pecans. Cover and chill the dough for about 30 minutes.

2 Preheat the oven to 400°F. With your hands, roll the dough into 1-inch balls. Place them about 1 inch apart on ungreased baking sheets. Bake until the cookies are set but not brown, about 10 minutes. Remove the cookies from the baking sheet and immediately roll them in the colored sugar. Let cool, roll in the sugar again, and serve.

mexican princess cinnamon tea cakes

MAKES 24 MINI TEA CAKES

Every time I make these little cakes, they disappear off the plate. Kids of all ages are fond of them because they literally melt in your mouth. For best results, bake them just before the party and serve them warm.

1 cup (2 sticks) unsalted butter, at room temperature

1½ cups sugar

1 large egg

1½ cups flour

¼ cup yellow cornmeal

1½ teaspoons baking powder

½ teaspoon salt

1 tablespoon plus ½ teaspoon ground cinnamon

½ cup milk or half-and-half

1 teaspoon pure alcohol-free vanilla extract

1 Preheat the oven to 350°F. Generously grease miniature muffin tins with oil or butter.

2 Put ½ cup of the butter and ½ cup of the sugar into the bowl of a food processor and process until light and fluffy. Add the egg and blend a few pulses. In a separate bowl, mix the flour, cornmeal, baking powder, salt, and ½ teaspoon cinnamon together. Alternately add the dry ingredients and the milk and vanilla to the butter mixture in three additions, processing until just mixed.

3 Fill the muffin tins about two-thirds full. Bake until golden brown, 10 to 12 minutes.

4 Meanwhile, mix the remaining 1 cup sugar and 1 tablespoon cinnamon together in a shallow bowl. Melt the remaining ½ cup butter and pour it into another shallow bowl. When the cakes are done, immediately remove them from the tins, and roll them in the melted butter and then in the cinnamon sugar. Let cool on a rack and serve slightly warm.

country garden lavender

PRINCESS TEA

France

IF POSSIBLE, HAVE THIS PARTY OUTSIDE
in or near a flower garden. Real or paper flowers and fluttering
butterflies set the scene. If your party needs to be inside,
use butterfly nets and pots of lavender to transform the room.
Purple lavender flowers on the table add aroma and beauty to
create a peaceful summery tea-party setting any time of year.

beverage suggestions

Lemon verbena tea or pink lemonade
Lavender Tea

costume suggestion

Pretty lavender or pink party dresses, patent-leather Mary Janes
or pink slippers. Lavender princesses wear their hair tied up
or back with a garland of flowers.

craft/activity

Make Butterflies

recipes

Cucumber Tulip Tea Sandwiches
Peanut Butterfly and Jelly Sandwiches
Lavender-Scented Whipped Cream and Blueberry Crêpes
Mini Lavender Cupcakes with Pastel Sprinkles

decorate the space

✖

Gather pretty pink, white, and lavender flowers from your garden (or make a quick purchase at the floral department at your grocery store) and arrange them in pastel vases. To give the room the feeling of a French country garden, use beautiful, aromatic pots of flowering lavender plants. Attach large paper butterflies overhead (from branches or the ceiling, if you're inside). Bring out your old-fashioned flowered dishes, teacups, and saucers for this special tea party.

make butterflies

Each princess will design the wings for her own butterfly. Be sure to remind the girls to make the wings mirror images of each other, using their creativity to incorporate all the little scraps of paper. If time is short, make the bodies of the butterflies before the party begins.

1 package 8½ by 11-inch multicolored construction paper (pastels for wings and darker colors for bodies)

6 pairs scissors

Colored pencils

Magic markers

3 packets of glitter

6 glue sticks, nontoxic glue, or cellophane tape

2 packages multicolored pipe cleaners

Hole punch and yarn, ribbon, or string (optional)

❶ To make the butterfly wings, choose a pastel sheet of construction paper. Fold the paper in half widthwise (5½ by 8½ inches) and draw an exaggerated letter B on it, using the fold as the straight line. Cut along the curves, discarding the outside part of the B or using it to decorate the wings. Encourage the princesses to draw on and decorate the wings with the colored pencils and markers, making the designs on one side mirror those on the other and using glitter on the edges.

❷ To make the butterfly body, use one piece of dark construction paper. The length of the body should be as long as the height of the wings. Cut the paper into four 2¾-by-8½-inch pieces; each section will be used for one body. Fold one piece of paper in half lengthwise. With scissors, round the corners on both ends of the paper.

The body now will be about 1¼ inches wide and 8 inches long. Opposite the folded side, about a quarter of the way from one end, make a rounded-wedge-shaped cut to create the head of the butterfly. Do not cut all the way through the fold. (At this point some girls may need help.) With the glue or tape, attach two pipe cleaners at the top of the head (curled at the ends) for antennae.

3 Place the folded edge of a body on the center fold of a pair of open decorated wings and glue.

4 If you'd like to hang the butterflies, make a hole with the punch on the upper edges of the wings. Thread the yarn through the holes, leaving a long loop in the middle. Knot the ends on the underside of the butterfly, and hang from the ceiling, a book shelf, or a curtain rod.

lavender tea

MAKES 1 QUART

The princesses will be delighted with the aromatic, subtle taste of lavender tea. Be sure to buy dried culinary lavender buds to make the tea, and brew extra for second servings. Do not use lavender from florists or garden centers, since it may have been treated with pesticides.

1 quart cold water

5 to 6 teaspoons dried culinary lavender buds

Clover honey or sugar (optional)

1 Bring the water to a boil and remove from the heat. Pour a splash of hot water into the teapot, swirl it around to warm the teapot, and then dump it out.

2 Spoon the lavender buds into the pot; pour hot water over the buds, cover, and steep for at least 5 minutes or to taste.

3 Serve using a tea strainer, with clover honey or sugar to taste.

cucumber tulip tea sandwiches

MAKES 12 OPEN-FACED SANDWICHES

Every little girl I know likes cucumbers, but if your princess hates cucumbers, thinly sliced carrots or radishes are good substitutes. Use a tulip or other flower-shaped 2- to 3-inch cookie cutter to cut out these pretty tea sandwiches.

12 thin slices white or whole-wheat bread

3 to 4 tablespoons unsalted butter, at room temperature

Pinch of sea salt

½ English or seedless cucumber, peeled and thinly sliced

1 Cut the bread into flower shapes and spread an even coat of soft butter all the way to the edges of the bread. Scatter a few grains of salt on the butter and top with the cucumber slices, trimming or overlapping to fit into the flower shape.

2 Transfer the sandwiches to a damp paper towel–lined tray or container, cover with another damp paper towel, then seal completely with plastic wrap and refrigerate until serving time.

peanut butterfly *and* jelly sandwiches

MAKES 6 BUTTERFLY SANDWICHES

To make these fanciful sandwiches, you can use 4-inch butterfly cookie cutters or simply cut the bread into free-form butterflies. If making them free-form, you may want to serve the sandwiches open-faced since the shapes may not perfectly match. If making open-faced sandwiches, just before serving, spread the peanut butter over the bread and top with jelly. Or, give the princesses the butterfly-shaped bread and let them make their own! If possible, choose organic peanut butter and naturally sweetened grape jelly to make these childhood favorites. For those with allergies, consider using organic soy nut butter—it's a good substitute.

12 thin slices white bread

One 16-ounce jar smooth peanut butter, preferably organic

One 8-ounce jar grape jelly, preferably naturally sweetened

1 Cut the bread into butterfly shapes and spread peanut butter over half of the slices. Spread grape jelly on the other half of the slices and top each peanut butter slice with a jelly slice.

2 Transfer the sandwiches to a tray, cover with plastic wrap, and set aside until serving time.

lavender-scented whipped cream
and blueberry crêpes

MAKES ABOUT 36 THREE-INCH OR 18 FIVE-INCH CRÊPES

Who doesn't like whipped cream? Delicate lavender-flavored cream and fresh blueberries are a simply delicious filling. Make the crêpes up to two weeks ahead of time and store them in the freezer. Defrost the crêpes in the refrigerator the day before serving. If making crêpes seems too time-consuming, they are also widely available in the frozen-food dessert section of most supermarkets.

CRÊPES

¾ cup milk

¾ cup cold water

3 egg yolks

1 tablespoon sugar

2 teaspoons pure alcohol-free vanilla extract

1½ cups sifted flour

5 tablespoons unsalted butter, melted

Vegetable oil for cooking

1 To prepare the crêpes, add the milk, water, egg yolks, sugar, vanilla, flour, and butter to the jar of a blender. Blend at top speed until smooth, about 1 minute. Cover and refrigerate overnight.

2 Brush a 5-inch crêpe pan or slant-sided skillet with oil and place over medium-high heat. When a drop of water skitters across the pan, it is ready to cook the crêpes.

3 Pour about 3 tablespoons of the batter into the middle of the crêpe pan; quickly tilt the pan back and forth until the batter creates a thin film on the bottom. Cook until the edges are light brown and the center is just set, about 60 seconds. Then slip the crêpe up onto the handle of the pan and flip it over, using your fingers or a thin little spatula, and cook the other side for about 30 seconds. Tip it out onto a paper towel. The first two or three you attempt may have holes and be messy. Just eat them, and by the time you get to the fourth or fifth one, you'll be a pro!

CREAM FILLING

1½ cups heavy whipping cream

1½ teaspoons dried culinary lavender buds, finely ground in a spice grinder

About 2 tablespoons sugar

1 teaspoon pure alcohol-free vanilla extract

2 pints fresh blueberries

Confectioners' sugar for dusting

4 Let the crêpes cool to room temperature and then store in a plastic bag in the refrigerator for up to 2 days, or freeze for up to 4 weeks. One day before the party, defrost in the refrigerator.

5 To prepare the cream filling: In a medium mixing bowl or the bowl of a stand mixer, mix the heavy cream, lavender, sugar, and vanilla and cover with plastic wrap. Refrigerate for at least 2 hours or up to 6 hours before whipping (and chill the mixer's beaters, too, for whipping the cream later).

6 Meanwhile, wash, pick over, and drain the blueberries. Reserve about ⅓ cup blueberries for garnish. When the filling mixture has been sufficiently chilled, whip until stiff peaks form, then taste and adjust the sweetness. Fold the blueberries into the cream and refrigerate for up to 1 hour before assembly.

7 Spoon about ¼ cup filling onto the bottom quarter of each crêpe and fold it in half, then in half again, to form a triangle. Arrange two crêpes on each plate and top with a dollop of blueberries and cream. Garnish the plates with a few blueberries, dust with confectioners' sugar, and serve at once.

mini lavender cupcakes *with* pastel sprinkles

MAKES 5 TO 6 DOZEN MINI CUPCAKES

Listen for signs of appreciation when you bring out a cupcake-filled plate dressed up with trailing ribbons. After baking the mini cupcakes, bake the rest of the batter in an 8-inch-square cake pan or regular-size muffin tins so your family may enjoy it.

CUPCAKES

3 cups sifted flour

1 teaspoon baking powder

1 teaspoon baking soda

½ teaspoon salt

¾ cup (1½ sticks) unsalted butter, at room temperature

2 cups sugar

4 large eggs

Grated zest of 1 lemon

2 tablespoons dried culinary lavender buds, finely ground in a spice grinder

1 tablespoon pure alcohol-free vanilla extract

1¼ cups plus 3 tablespoons buttermilk

continued . . .

1 To prepare the cupcakes, preheat the oven to 350°F. Generously grease the mini muffin tins with oil or line with paper liners.

2 Sift the flour, baking powder, baking soda, and salt together into a medium mixing bowl and set aside. In another large mixing bowl, cream the butter until smooth. Gradually add the sugar and continue beating until light and fluffy. Add the eggs one at a time, beating well after each addition. Beat in the lemon zest, lavender, and vanilla. Starting with dry ingredients, alternate adding the flour mixture and the buttermilk in three additions, beating well after each addition.

3 Fill the muffin tins about three-quarters full. Bake until the tops are golden and the cakes spring back to the touch, 10 to 12 minutes. Let cool in the pan on a wire rack for 10 minutes. Tip the cupcakes onto the rack and let cool completely.

ICING

One 8-ounce package cream cheese,
at room temperature

1 cup (2 sticks) unsalted butter,
at room temperature

1 tablespoon dried culinary
lavender buds, finely ground
in a spice grinder

1 tablespoon pure alcohol-free
vanilla extract

Pinch of salt

4 cups confectioners' sugar

Lavender-colored sugar
or sprinkles for decorating
Yellow and lavender ribbons for
decorating the cake plate

4 To prepare the icing: Beat the cream cheese and butter together in a medium mixing bowl until light and fluffy. Mix in the lavender, vanilla, and salt. With the beaters running, gradually add the confectioners' sugar and continue beating until smooth. This icing may be made ahead of time—just cover with plastic wrap and refrigerate. Bring to room temperature before icing the cupcakes.

5 Fill a star-tipped pastry bag with icing and pipe it onto the cupcakes. Sprinkle with the lavender-colored sugar and arrange on a platter. Refrigerate for about 20 minutes to firm up the icing. When ready to serve, tuck strands of ribbons under the cupcakes so they dangle as streamers over the edges of the platter.

indian

PRINCESS TEA

India

IN THIS SOUTHEAST ASIAN ROYAL PALACE ENVIRONMENT, you can almost feel the breezes from the Indian Ocean. Princesses enter through beaded curtains into a dimly lit room with sitar or flute music playing softly in the background. If you have an overhead fan, use it to add a gentle breeze and complete this setting. Bejeweled Indian princesses savor Indian delicacies and sip spiced or chocolate chai.

beverage suggestions

Apple-mango juice
India Spiced Chai
Hot Chocolate Chai

costume suggestion

Silky slacks with saris or silk wraps, gold or silver slippers,
silk scarves over head and face, and brass jewelry

craft/activity

Make Jewelry

recipes

Chicken Satay with Peanut Dipping Sauce
Stuffed Baked-Potato Princesses
Cardamom-Scented Rice Pudding
Cinnamon Coins

decorate the space

·❖·

Hang beaded curtains in the doorway to the party. Use rich gold or red silk scarves or gold-painted fabric to cover low tables. Add bowls of gold-wrapped chocolate coins and bowls of cool water with red and yellow rose petals floating in them. Toss vibrant colored cushions or chair seats on the floor.

make jewelry

❖

No princess ever has enough jewelry, so girls will love making their own neck-laces and bracelets. The girls can put various beads in egg carton cups and use the open lid as a place to lay out beads while stringing them. Various packaged jewelry kits are also available, and if this seems easier to you, buy one for each princess. Otherwise, you should be able to find the materials for this project at a crafts or bead store.

6 egg cartons

300 assorted colors and sizes of beads and spacers

Measuring tape

Scissors

3 packages 1-mm lamé or Stretch Magic Clear elastic line

Long-nose pliers

6 medium lobster-claw clasps and 6 oval clasps, for closures

1 Fill the clean egg cartons with various beads and set them on the table for the princesses.

2 Using the measuring tape and scissors, help the princesses measure the lengths of line or clear wires necessary for a necklace or bracelet, then help them string different beads onto their strings.

3 After the beads are strung, use the pliers to attach the closure clasps. Assist each girl in putting on her jewelry to wear for the rest of the party and to take home.

india spiced chai

MAKES 1 QUART

In India, families enjoy a sweet milky black tea flavored with cloves, cinnamon, ginger, and cardamom at breakfast, along with fruit. The delightful combination of herbs and spices already measured out into tea bags makes it so easy to enjoy at a party like this. Granulated sugar is the customary sweetener, but I prefer the flavor of clover blossom honey.

2 chai tea bags, such as
India Spice Teahouse Chai

1 quart boiling water

4 tablespoons honey

About 8 tablespoons
hot or cold milk

1 Place the tea bags in the teapot and pour the boiling water over. Let steep for 5 minutes.

2 To serve hot, add 1 tablespoon of honey to each teacup and fill two-thirds full with tea, add hot milk to taste, and stir.

3 To serve cold, stir honey into the hot tea to taste, and bring it to room temperature. Transfer it to a glass jar and cover and refrigerate until serving time. When serving, pour tea into glasses and add cold milk to taste.

Hot Chocolate Chai

Chocolate chai tea is cloudy, but the aroma and taste are clearly delightful. Adding a hint of cocoa to loose tea leaves in the pot is the magic formula that will have princesses asking for more. Have a small pitcher of warm milk and a bowl of sugar for each princess to add as much as she likes. I add a little sugar to my cup, no milk, and stir it with chocolate sticks found in sweet shops or candy stores.

2 tablespoons chai tea leaves

1 teaspoon unsweetend cocoa

1 quart boiling water

Sugar and warm milk as desired

Chocolate stirrers

1 Place the tea leaves and cocoa in the teapot and pour the boiling water over. Let steep for 5 minutes.

2 To serve, add 1 teaspoon of sugar to each teacup and fill two-thirds full with tea. Add warm milk to taste and stir with the chocolate stirrers.

chicken satay with peanut dipping sauce

MAKES 6 SERVINGS

Make the dipping sauce for this recipe a few days ahead to save time. The recipe is equally as tasty if you substitute beef or pork for the chicken. If you need a substitute for peanut butter, soy-nut butter works well for the sauce. You normally can find short wooden skewers at the supermarket.

1 cup plain yogurt

2 boneless skinless chicken breasts, trimmed

18 to 24 four-inch wooden skewers, soaked in warm water for at least 2 hours

MARINADE

1 cup unsweetened coconut milk

1 teaspoon peeled chopped fresh ginger root

2 teaspoons curry powder

1 clove garlic, minced

2 tablespoons fresh lime juice

¼ cup hot water

1 One day ahead of time, put the yogurt in a shallow bowl, roll the chicken in it, cover with plastic wrap, and refrigerate overnight to tenderize the meat. On the day of the party, remove the chicken from the yogurt and pat dry, cut into small bite-sized pieces, and thread two or three pieces onto the wooden skewers.

2 To prepare the marinade: In a bowl, whisk together the coconut milk, ginger, curry powder, garlic, lime juice, and hot water. Pour the mixture over the skewered chicken and let marinate for 30 minutes or up to 2 hours before cooking.

3 Preheat the broiler to high or the oven to 450°F. Arrange the skewered chicken on a foil-lined broiler pan or baking sheet and broil or bake until the chicken is light brown on the edges and cooked, 4 to 8 minutes. The cooking time will depend on the size of the chicken. Remove from the heat and let cool for 5 minutes or until at room temperature.

PEANUT DIPPING SAUCE

⅓ cup smooth peanut butter,
preferably organic

2 tablespoons fresh lime juice

2 tablespoons soy sauce

About 1 teaspoon sugar

1 clove garlic, minced (optional)

About ⅓ cup hot water

4 To prepare the dipping sauce: Whisk the peanut butter with the lime juice, soy sauce, sugar, and garlic (if using) until smooth. Stir in the hot water, adding more if the sauce seems too thick, taste, and adjust the seasonings.

5 Serve the chicken with a few tablespoons of the dipping sauce in the center of the plate.

stuffed baked-potato princesses

MAKES 6 SERVINGS

Kids love twice-baked potatoes, and the girls will be delighted when they see these potatoes made into stuffed princesses with vegetable faces. You'll love them too, since the potatoes are done before the party. Simply attach the hair and arms just before serving. When shopping for ingredients, look for uniformly sized potatoes.

6 large Idaho baking potatoes

4 to 5 tablespoons unsalted butter

1 cup heavy cream or milk

1 or 2 large red bell peppers,
cut in half and seeded

1 small green bell pepper,
cut in half and seeded

1 large carrot, peeled
and cooked whole

Sea salt

Fresh ground white pepper

1 bunch curly parsley for garnish

1 Preheat the oven to 400°F. Scrub the potatoes, poke two or three holes in the skins, place on a baking sheet, and bake until they are soft to the point of a table fork, about 1 hour.

2 Meanwhile, in a saucepan over moderate heat, melt the butter in the cream. Keep hot.

3 Cut the red bell pepper into 12 tulip shapes to use for hands and 6 thin strips to use for mouths. Cut the green bell pepper into tiny squares for eyes. Cut the carrot into ⅛-inch-thick slices to make the potato princesses' faces.

4 When the potatoes are baked and cool enough to handle, cut a small slice off the largest end of each potato so you can stand it upright. (Reserve this piece.) Then cut off about one-quarter of the opposite end and carefully scoop the insides into a large mixing bowl. Add the butter-cream mixture and mash the potatoes until smooth with a potato masher or the beaters of electric mixer. Season with salt and pepper.

5 Fill a pastry bag with mashed potatoes and fill the empty potato skins with the filling (or use a spoon). Mound the filling slightly above the skins to form a neck where you'll attach the face. Place the small circle cut from the bottom of the potato skin as a cap on the back of the mashed potatoes.

6 With toothpicks, attach green-pepper squares to each carrot slice for eyes and a strip of red pepper to the carrot for the mouth. (Use round wooden toothpicks to attach the facial features on the potato, breaking or snipping off the ends of toothpicks that stick out.) Attach the carrot face to the potato body with the mashed potatoes. Hold until serving time. Reheat the potatoes in a 350°F oven for about 10 minutes.

7 Just before serving, arrange the parsley leaves around the top of the faces as hair. Using toothpicks as arms, spear the red pepper pieces, and attach to the potato body. Serve immediately.

cardamom-scented rice pudding

MAKES ABOUT 8 SERVINGS

Indian cooks traditionally use long-grain rice for this recipe, but for an extra creamy consistency, use short-grain arborio rice. Coconut milk, cinnamon, and cardamom pods, often found in chai tea, add a gentle exotic scent and flavor to this favorite childhood dessert. Use ramekins, custard cups, or pretty teacups for a festive presentation.

2 cups water

1 cup arborio or other short-grain white rice

¼ teaspoon salt

2 teaspoons unsalted butter

1 cinnamon stick

2 cups unsweetened coconut milk

1 cup rice milk

⅓ cup sugar

1 tablespoon pure alcohol-free vanilla extract

1 cardamom pod, cracked

Ground cinnamon for sprinkling

1 In a saucepan over medium-high heat, bring the water to a boil; add the rice, salt, butter, and cinnamon stick. Reduce the heat to a simmer and cook for 20 minutes.

2 Add the coconut milk, rice milk, sugar, vanilla, and cardamom pod to the rice and bring to a boil. Taste and adjust for sweetness. Then transfer the mixture to the top of a double boiler set over simmering water. Cover and cook until tender, about 45 minutes. Remove the cinnamon stick and cardamom pod and spoon the pudding into ramekins. Let cool to room temperature. The mixture will thicken as it cools. Sprinkle cinnamon on top of the pudding and serve.

cinnamon coins

These sweet, buttery cookies are especially yummy with Hot Chocolate Chai (page 79). Bake them up to 2 weeks before the party and store in an airtight container.

½ cup (1 stick) unsalted butter, at room temperature

¾ cup plus 2 tablespoons sugar

3 teaspoons ground cinnamon

¼ teaspoon ground cardamom

1 teaspoon pure alcohol-free vanilla extract

1 large egg

1¼ cups flour

1½ teaspoons baking powder

½ teaspoon salt

Light cream for brushing

1 In the bowl of an electric mixer, beat the butter until fluffy. Add the ¾ cup sugar and continue beating until light and fluffy. Stir in 2 teaspoons of the cinnamon, the cardamom, and vanilla. Add the egg and beat well. In a separate small bowl, mix the flour, baking powder, and salt together, then add to the butter mixture and blend. Cover with plastic wrap and chill until the dough is firm.

2 On a floured board, roll the dough into two logs about 1½ inches thick, wrap in plastic, and refrigerate overnight or until ready to bake.

3 Preheat the oven to 350°F. Line two baking sheets with parchment paper.

4 Mix the remaining 1 teaspoon cinnamon and 2 tablespoons sugar together and set aside for sprinkling. Cut the logs into ¼-inch-thick slices and transfer to the prepared baking sheets, placing them about 1 inch apart. Brush the tops with cream and sprinkle with the cinnamon-sugar mixture.

5 Bake until no imprint remains when you touch the tops of the cookies lightly and the edges are barely colored, 10 to 14 minutes. Transfer to a wire rack and let cool completely before serving.

african

PRINCESS TEA

✹

Africa

ENTER INTO A JUNGLE OF STUFFED ANIMALS
set around a tented room that could be anywhere on the African
continent. Drumbeats are significant in the African music playing
softly in the background, and earth-toned and animal-print fabric
draped over chairs and floor pillows evoke an informal gathering space
for little girls. Even though many wild animals surround this party,
it's safe for the princesses to drink tea, eat casual finger food and
sweets, and weave their own baskets.

beverage suggestions

Lemon Zinger Tea
Chamomile tea
Grape-Apple Juice

costume suggestion

Bright patterned cotton wrap-around skirts with a top or African sarongs
with a matching headscarf or braided hair. Add lots and lots of colorful arm
and ankle bangle bracelets, but bare feet or sandals are appropriate.

craft/activity

Basket Weaving

recipes

Egg Pockets
Sesame-Roasted Red Potatoes with Yogurt Cucumber Dip
Mini Malva Puddings with Coconut Sauce
Maandazi (Sugared Doughnuts)

decorate the space

✽

Drape large white sheets from the ceiling to the corners of the room to create a tent in the jungle. Fill the room with as many stuffed animals as possible—wild animals are preferable but any kind will do just fine. Throw earth-toned printed fabrics over the chairs, arrange animal-print pillows and scarves attractively around the room, and add clay jugs or bowls of protea (South Africa's national flower) and tall, colorful cannas or gladiolus. Pass out boxes of animal cookies as take-home party favors.

basket weaving

❁

Little girls love to keep their treasures and carry their stuff in baskets. For generations African women have passed down the art form of weaving twigs, straw, fabrics, and paper into baskets. Before the party, make a sample basket for the girls to examine while they weave their own. Help the younger princesses with the first few steps, then they will quickly master the weaving. Don't forget the video camera!

Ruler

Pencil

Scissors

Two 8½-by-11-inch sheets colored heavyweight art paper, per guest (with a few extra for mistakes)—a good color combination is black, brown, red, and beige

Clear nontoxic glue

2 bags of 5½-by-⅓-inch skinny sticks

One 6-inch cake cardboard circle per guest (with a few extra for mistakes) or heavy-duty paper plates

Double-stick tape

Cellophane tape

1 roll of paper towels per guest for support during weaving

2 rolls of colored raffia

Box of paper clips

1 Using the ruler, pencil, and scissors, cut each sheet of colored paper into 1-inch-long-by-11-inch-wide strips.

2 Glue one skinny stick at a time down the center of each strip and let dry for few minutes. Be sure to leave a 3-inch space at the bottom of each strip. The 3-inch end of the strips will be attached to the cardboard circle, which will be the bottom of the basket. (Sticks are for support.)

3 Before gluing the 11-inch-long strips, make sure the sticks rest right at the edge of the cardboard round and fold the strip at that point.

4 Use double-stick tape to attach the strips to the cardboard. The stick strip must be facedown on the cardboard circle. Place one strip at a time around the cardboard, with ½ inch between the strips. Fan them out evenly to look like a star. Reinforce the strips with glue or cellophane tape. (Let the glue set up for a few minutes.)

5 Turn the basket upside down on a roll of paper towels to begin weaving.

6 Tie a knot on the end of the raffia. Tape it horizontally across the bottom of a strip. (This will become the sides of the basket.) Weave the raffia over and under all of the strips. Cut the raffia and tie both ends together, and tape them to the paper. Repeat one more time with the basket upside down. Remove the paper towel roll and turn the basket right-side up. Using the same technique, finish weaving until it is a basket.

7 When the weaving is completed, trim the strips to an even height. Fold the ends from the outside in to form a rim, secure with glue, and hold them together with paper clips until the glue dries.

lemon zinger tea

MAKES 1 QUART

Use two cinnamon sticks to flavor the water before adding the tea bags and six more for stirrers. This tea is delicious as is, but some princesses may take theirs with milk.

8 cinnamon sticks

1 quart boiling water

4 Lemon Zinger tea bags

Sugar cubes or honey to taste

1 Place 2 cinnamon sticks in the teapot, pour the boiling water over them, and let steep for 5 to 8 minutes. Remove the cinnamon sticks and add the tea bags. Cover the pot, and let steep for 5 to 8 minutes longer. Remove the tea bags and discard.

2 Add sugar or honey to the cup, place a fresh cinnamon stick in the cup, and pour in the tea. Stir with the cinnamon stick until the sugar is dissolved.

grape-apple juice

MAKES 2 QUARTS

Combining grape with apple juice enhances both, but if you prefer, serve plain grape juice. Use your favorite brand to make this festive drink.

1 quart apple juice

1 quart grape juice

1 or 2 sprigs fresh mint

1 Mix the apple and grape juices together and stir to blend. Add mint and chill until serving time. Remove the mint before serving.

egg pockets

Street carts serving finger food are found in every African city. Eggs are common but African breads are regional, varying from a baguette, corn bread, crisp flat bread, soft crêpe, and naan to pita bread. For this party I chose pita pockets because they are available in every market. Cutting the pockets into quarters makes it easy for little fingers to hold.

⅓ cup mayonnaise

¼ teaspoon chili powder

1 teaspoon fresh squeezed lime juice, or more to taste

8 eggs

¾ cup half-and-half or milk

1 teaspoon salt

2 pinches, freshly ground black pepper, or more to taste

3 tablespoons olive or canola oil

½ cup diced red onion

Six 4-inch whole-wheat pita breads, split

⅓ head iceberg lettuce, shredded

2 plum tomatoes, thinly sliced

1 In a small mixing bowl, whisk together the mayonnaise, chili powder, and lime juice until blended. Taste and adjust the seasoning and set aside.

2 In a small bowl, whisk the eggs, half-and-half, salt, and pepper together until blended. Set a small nonstick sauté pan over high heat and generously coat the bottom with the oil. Working in batches, add one-third of the red onion and sauté for 30 to 40 seconds until soft, then pour about one-third of the egg mixture into the skillet and cook until set on the bottom. Gently loosen the eggs around the edges, then shake the pan to loosen the bottom. Continue cooking until golden brown on the bottom and completely cooked through. Holding a plate over the skillet, tip eggs out of the pan onto the plate, and repeat with the remaining onion and eggs.

3 Spread a thin layer of the mayonnaise mixture on one side of each pita pocket. Cut the eggs in half and stuff both pita halves with a layer of eggs. Add lettuce and tomato, cut pockets in half, and arrange four pockets on each plate.

sesame-roasted red potatoes
with yogurt cucumber dip

MAKES 6 SERVINGS

Roasting little potatoes makes them taste sweeter than boiled potatoes. No forks are necessary because the princesses will use toothpicks to dip their potatoes into the yogurt cucumber dip.

24 small (1-to 2-inch) red potatoes, scrubbed, cut into bite-sized pieces

About 2 tablespoons extra-virgin olive oil

1½ tablespoons toasted sesame seeds

YOGURT CUCUMBER DIP

1 cup plain nonfat yogurt "cheese"

⅔ cup minced cucumber

¼ cup minced red onion

2 tablespoons chopped flat-leaf (Italian) parsley

2 tablespoons chopped mint leaves, plus white leaves for garnish

½ teaspoon ground coriander

½ teaspoon ground cardamom

Pinch of salt

Pinch of freshly ground black pepper

2 teaspoons fresh lime juice

1 Preheat the oven to 400° F.

2 Coat the bottom of a baking dish large enough to hold all the potatoes in one layer with olive oil. Roll the potatoes in the oil, drizzling more to lightly coat them if necessary. Scatter sesame seeds over the potatoes.

3 Bake until the potatoes are light brown on the edges and tender to the point of a knife, 20 to 25 minutes. Remove from the oven and let cool to room temperature.

4 To make the dip: In a bowl, whisk the yogurt cheese with the cucumber, onion, parsley, mint, coriander, cardamom, salt, pepper, and lime juice until blended. Taste and adjust the seasonings. Spoon the dip into a ramekin and refrigerate until serving time.

Note If you're unable to find yogurt "cheese," you can easily make your own by putting a quart of plain yogurt into a strainer lined with a damp cheesecloth set over a bowl. Cover with plastic wrap and refrigerate overnight. Discard the liquid "whey" in the bottom of the bowl and store the "cheese" in a plastic container in the refrigerator.

mini malva puddings *with* coconut sauce

MAKES ABOUT 24 MINI PUDDINGS

This sweet dessert represents the Dutch influence in South African cuisine. The characteristic indent in the center of the pudding that forms at the end of the baking time is the perfect spot to pour the coconut sauce into. Bake the puddings in mini muffin tins ahead of time, then just before serving, reheat them in the oven for the best taste.

PUDDING

1 egg

1 cup dark brown sugar

1 teaspoon pure alcohol-free vanilla extract

1 tablespoon strawberry jam

1 cup unbleached flour

1 teaspoon baking soda

¼ teaspoon salt

1 tablespoon plus 1 teaspoon unsalted butter

1 teaspoon white balsamic vinegar

1 cup milk

1 To prepare the puddings: Place a rack in the middle of the oven and preheat to 350°F. Generously grease the mini muffin pans with butter or spray with oil.

2 In a mixing bowl, beat the egg with the brown sugar until it is light and thick, about 4 minutes. Add the vanilla and the strawberry jam and blend well. Sift the flour together with baking soda and salt, and place in a bowl. Melt the butter and vinegar together, and stir in the milk. Add the dry ingredients to the egg mixture alternately with the milk-butter mixture, beating well after each addition.

3 Fill the prepared pans one-half to two-thirds full with batter. Bake until the puddings are puffed and brown on top, resist when pressed with a finger, and a toothpick inserted into the center comes out clean, 15 to 18 minutes. Remove from the oven and place on a rack set on a sided baking sheet to catch the drips when you add the sauce.

COCONUT SAUCE

⅔ cup unsweetened coconut milk,
thick top part

½ cup granulated sugar

1 teaspoon pure alcohol-free
vanilla extract

3 ounces unsalted butter, melted

Fresh strawberries, sliced, for garnish

4 To prepare the sauce: In a mixing bowl, whisk the coconut milk with the sugar until blended. Add the vanilla and butter and set aside.

5 Slowly pour the sauce into the center of the hot puddings and let it soak into the puddings. Continue pouring the sauce on the hot puddings until they are saturated, 15 to 20 minutes.

6 Tip the puddings onto the drip pan and transfer to a pretty platter or small dessert plates. Garnish each pudding with a slice of strawberry on top.

Note *To make ahead and reheat*—Cover the room-temperature, saturated puddings with plastic wrap and refrigerate. Reheat in 350°F oven for 10 to 15 minutes before serving. Garnish with the strawberry slices.

maandazi (sugared doughnuts)

MAKES ABOUT 20 DOUGHNUTS

East African children love these doughnuts that are a cousin to the *koesisters* from South Africa. Rolling the hot doughnuts in the cinnamon and sugar gives the *maandazi* a spicy, sweet coating. If made ahead, gently reheat in the oven until they are warm and reroll them just before serving.

2 cups all-purpose flour

2 teaspoons baking powder

⅓ cup brown sugar

½ teaspoon salt

¼ teaspoon ground cardamom

1 egg, beaten

¾ cup milk or half-and-half

¼ cup unsalted butter, melted

1 teaspoon pure alcohol-free
vanilla extract

⅔ cup confectioners' sugar

1½ teaspoons ground cinnamon

¼ teaspoon freshly grated nutmeg

About 1 quart canola oil for frying

1 In a large mixing bowl, stir the flour, baking powder, sugar, salt, and cardamom together until evenly blended. In a small bowl, whisk the egg and add the milk, butter, and vanilla and blend.

2 Make a well in the center of the dry ingredients and pour the liquid ingredients into the center. With a fork, stir the mixture together until it forms a soft dough. If it seems too sticky, add a little flour. Cover the bowl with a damp towel or plastic wrap and let rise for 30 to 40 minutes, until the dough is light.

3 Stir the confectioners' sugar, cinnamon, and nutmeg in a small shallow bowl until blended; set aside.

4 Fill a deep-fryer or deep, heavy pot (cast iron) over high heat with enough oil to come three inches up the sides of the pot and heat the oil until it reaches 350°F. Line a pan with several layers of paper towels and place it next to the pot.

5 Turn the dough onto a lightly floured surface and roll out to a rectangle about ½ inch thick. Dip a cookie cutter into the flour and cut the dough into 2-inch rounds. Transfer the rounds to a baking sheet. Reroll the scraps of dough until all of the dough is cut. Poke a hole in the center of each doughnut with your thumb or finger as you carefully drop it into the oil.

6 Working in batches, fry about 4 doughnuts at a time. Turn the dough several times to brown, 3 to 4 minutes total. With a slotted spoon, transfer the doughnuts to the lined pan to drain for about 2 minutes, or until cool enough to handle. Immediately roll them in the cinnamon-sugar mixture and let cool on a rack. Serve warm or at room temperature.

fairy

PRINCESS TEA

★

Fairyland

A FAIRY PRINCESS PARTY IS THE PLACE TO MAKE
as many dreams as possible come true. Crown each princess
with a tiara and give her a magic wand upon arrival and let the
bewitchment begin. After the princesses eat enchanting foods,
they will tell fairy tales to feed their young imaginations.
Background music of gentle tinkling chimes or bells, along
with hanging twinkling fairy wings and fanciful tiny pink
and white flowers, enhance the fairyland atmosphere.

beverage suggestions
Berri-Good or berry bunch tea
Strawberry Lemonade

✦

costume suggestion
Pretty party dresses or flowing skirts, satin or patent slippers,
and hair festooned with flowers and ribbons

✦

craft/activity
Make Fairy-Tale Books
Make Magic Mirrors
Tell stories

✦

recipes
Angel Wing Turkey Croissants
Airy Egg-Salad Cream Puffs
Magical Fairy-Dusted Brownies
Good Fairy Pink Strawberry and Cream Meringues

decorate the space

✦

Cover the table with pink or pastel silk or satin fabric. For a centerpiece, make a wishing well for the princesses' penny wishes. Or make a castle out of construction paper and stand it on a mirror or on a sea of blue construction paper to suggest water surrounding the castle. Fill miniature glass slippers with pink lollipops and pink pastel candies. Hang fairy wings and pink veils from the ceiling and scatter sparkling fallen stars in green paper grass below.

make fairy-tale books

★

Princesses who love to write stories can publish their own fairy-tale book. The outside cover should read "Once Upon a Time . . . by (name of princess)," but the interior is totally up to the author. Be prepared for remarkable fantasies!

Colored construction paper

Unlined white paper

Pens or pencils

Hole punch

Box of paper hole protectors

Colored yarn, ribbons, or string to bind the books together

1 Make book covers from one piece of folded colored construction paper. Preprint "Once Upon a Time . . ." on the outside front cover.

2 Make the inside pages from three pieces of white paper folded the same size as or slightly smaller than the cover. If desired, print the skeleton of a story on the white paper and the girls can fill in the blanks to complete the story.

3 Punch two holes along the crease of the paper (it works best to make the holes through all the sheets of paper at the same time). Attach a hole protector to each hole to prevent the yarn from tearing the binding. From the outside cover, thread the yarn through the holes. Knot the yarn on the outside to bind the book together. The princesses can then read their stories to each other in the storytelling area.

make magic mirrors
★

Decorate hand mirrors with silver glitter and fairy-dust confetti. In the storytelling area, you can place a larger mirror on the floor, hiding the frame or edges with silk or paper leaves or netting. This is the gathering point for the princesses to tell their own imaginary stories. Be prepared for very tall fairy tales!

6 unbreakable hand mirrors

6 glitter glue sticks

1 package silver glitter

1 package gold glitter

2 packages assorted sized stars

24 pastel streamers

1. Instruct each girl to decorate her mirror with glue, glitter, and stars around the edges.

2. Glue the streamers on top for effective waving.

recipes

strawberry lemonade

To save time, stir strawberry purée into the lemonade and refrigerate before the party.

One 10-ounce package frozen sweetened strawberries, thawed, or one 8-ounce bottle strawberry flavored syrup

2 quarts lemonade

1 Purée the berries and their juices in the blender. Pour lemonade into a large pitcher, and whisk about 1 cup of the purée or ½ cup of the strawberry syrup into the lemonade until it looks pink. Taste and adjust the sweetness by adding more strawberries or syrup, if desired. Store in the refrigerator until serving time.

angel wing turkey croissants

MAKES 6 SANDWICHES

Pick up fresh or frozen croissants at the bakery or supermarket. Follow the directions on the package to bake. To create an angel, you'll cut the finished turkey-filled croissants in half to form wings on a plate, and use the Airy Egg-Salad Cream puffs for the bodies.

6 croissants

About ¼ cup mayonnaise
or soft butter

6 to 8 slices roast turkey,
cut to fit the croissants

6 green leaf lettuce leaves,
cut to fit the croissants

6 Airy Egg-Salad Cream Puffs
(page 108)

6 cherry tomatoes

12 small sweet pickles

1   Cut each croissant in half horizontally, spread a thin layer of mayonnaise inside, add the turkey and lettuce, and replace the croissant top to make the sandwich.

2   Cut the sandwich in half across the middle. Arrange the halves in wing fashion on individual plates. Place an egg-salad cream puff between the wings to form the body. Add a cherry tomato on top for a head and 2 sweet pickles for legs to form an angel.

airy egg-salad cream puffs

MAKES 12 THREE-INCH CREAM PUFFS AND ABOUT 2½ CUPS EGG SALAD

Make the egg salad for this recipe a day or two ahead, leaving plenty of time to set up on the day of the party. Bake these light-as-a-feather cream puffs early in the day. Store them in a turned-off oven. If the notion of making cream puffs is daunting, either buy them from a local bakery or substitute small soft rolls.

EGG SALAD

8 eggs, preferably organic

Sea salt

Freshly ground black pepper

½ teaspoon Dijon mustard

About 3 tablespoons mayonnaise

1 stalk celery, peeled and minced (optional)

2 scallions, minced (optional)

1 tablespoon chopped fresh parsley (optional)

1 To prepare the egg salad: Place the eggs in a large pot with enough cold water to cover them by 2 inches. Cover the pot and bring to a boil over high heat. Boil for only 1 minute. Turn off the heat and let the eggs stand in the hot water for 10 minutes. Drain the hot water off, and immediately run cold water over the eggs to stop the cooking process. Crack the shells of the eggs on the side of the pot. Let the eggs stand in the cold water until they are cool enough to handle, 10 to 15 minutes. Carefully peel off the shells.

2 Chop the eggs, transfer them to a mixing bowl, and season with salt and pepper.

3 In a small bowl, stir the mustard into the mayonnaise until well blended. Add just enough of the mayonnaise mixture to the eggs to bind them. Stir in the celery, scallions, and parsley (if using). Taste and adjust the seasonings. Cover with plastic wrap and refrigerate until assembly.

4 To prepare the cream puffs: Preheat the oven to 425°F. Line two baking sheets with parchment paper.

CREAM PUFFS

1 cup water

½ cup (1 stick) unsalted butter, cold,
cut into pieces

½ teaspoon salt

About ⅛ teaspoon freshly grated
nutmeg

1 cup sifted all-purpose flour

4 large eggs

Egg wash (1 egg, beaten with
1 tablespoon cold water)

5 In a saucepan over high heat, bring the water, butter, salt, and nutmeg to a boil. Cook until the butter is melted, about 1 minute. Remove the pan from the heat, pour in the flour all at once, and beat with a wooden spoon until smooth. Set the pan back on moderate heat and beat the mixture until it leaves the sides of the pan and forms a ball, about 3 minutes. Transfer the mixture to the bowl of an electric mixer. With the beaters running at high speed, add the eggs one at a time, beating well after each addition until smooth, about 3 minutes longer.

3 Fill a star-tipped pastry bag with the choux paste and pipe six 2½- to 3-inch circles onto the prepared baking sheets about 2 inches apart. Pipe another circle just inside the first circles, and then another inside that, filling the center and forming the puff. Lightly brush the tops with the egg wash. Place in the preheated oven and bake for 15 minutes until puffed and brown. Remove the pan from the oven and make a small slit in the side of each puff with a small knife. Return the cream puffs to the oven and bake for 5 minutes longer. Turn off the oven and leave the puffs in the oven with the door ajar for 10 minutes. Remove from the oven. When cool enough to handle, cut each cream puff in half horizontally. With your fingers or a fork, carefully pull out any uncooked dough inside and discard. Let cool on a rack.

4 Remove the tops of the cream puffs, spoon 3 or 4 tablespoonfuls of the egg salad into the bottoms, and replace the tops.

magical fairy-dusted brownies

These brownies are magical because they melt in your mouth almost like fudge. Sprinkle confectioners' sugar on top for fairy dust, and serve them on a silver doily–lined plate. Of course you can buy a brownie mix, but these are very easy to make from scratch!

1 cup (2 sticks) unsalted butter

2 cups granulated sugar

¼ cup unsweetened cocoa powder

4 eggs

1 tablespoon pure alcohol-free vanilla extract

1½ cups flour

1 teaspoon salt

Confectioners' sugar for dusting

1 Preheat the oven to 375°F. Generously grease and flour an 11-by-17-inch jelly-roll pan.

2 In a small saucepan over low heat, melt the butter and stir in the sugar and cocoa powder until dissolved. Remove from the heat and let cool, about 10 minutes.

3 Working with a wooden spoon and a mixing bowl, beat the eggs with the vanilla. Beat in the butter-cocoa mixture. Sift the flour together with the salt and stir into the batter until just blended.

4 Pour into the prepared pan and spread out evenly. Bake until the top is dull looking and a toothpick barely comes out clean, 20 to 25 minutes.

5 Remove from the oven, dust with confectioners' sugar, and let cool on a rack. Cut into squares when cool and dust with confectioners' sugar again just before serving.

good fairy pink strawberry
and cream meringues

This dessert is everything sweet and pretty. The berries and whipped cream make a natural pink confection that all kids love. If there's no time to bake, it's perfectly fine to order meringues from the local bakery.

MERINGUES

4 to 6 large egg whites

Pinch of salt

1 cup granulated sugar

1 teaspoon pure alcohol-free vanilla extract

1. To prepare the meringues: Preheat the oven to 250°F. Line two baking sheets with parchment paper.

2. In a spotless electric mixer bowl, beat the egg whites with the salt until frothy, about 2 minutes. With the beaters running, add the sugar 2 tablespoons at a time, scraping down the sides of the bowl every so often. Continue beating until very stiff peaks form and it looks satiny, 8 to 10 minutes.

3. Fill a pastry bag fitted with a star tip with the meringue, and pipe twelve 3-inch circles onto the prepared baking sheets, about 2 inches apart. Then pipe another ring on the outer edges of the circles to form an edible dish that will hold the berries and cream. You may also drop 2 or 3 spoonfuls of meringue onto the prepared baking sheet, about 2 inches apart, and then with the back of a wet tablespoon, make an indent in the center to form a dish.

FILLING

2 cups (1 pint) heavy whipping cream

About 2 tablespoons
confectioners' sugar

1½ teaspoons pure alcohol-free
vanilla extract

1 quart fresh strawberries, stems
removed, washed and patted dry;
reserve 12 perfect strawberries
for garnish

About ¼ cup sugar, honey,
or agave syrup

4 Place the meringues on the center rack of the oven and bake until they are set and pale almond in color, about 1½ hours. Turn off the oven. Leave the meringues in the oven 30 minutes longer. Remove from the oven and let cool completely on a rack. With a thin pancake turner, carefully slip the meringues off the paper and store them in an airtight container until ready to serve.

5 To prepare the filling: In a cold mixing bowl, beat the heavy cream, confectioners' sugar, and vanilla until thick, about 4 minutes. Cover and refrigerate until assembly.

6 Slice the 1 quart strawberries into a large bowl, sprinkle the sugar over, gently stir, and let stand for 10 to 20 minutes. Taste and adjust the sweetness. Set aside until ready to assemble.

7 If there's more than ¼ cup of berry juice accumulated in the bottom of the bowl, pour it off and add it to the lemonade (page 106). Fold the berries into the whipped cream and fill the meringues. Garnish each with a perfect strawberry and serve at once.

source list

food

Fortune Cookies

Creative-Cookies
818-493-0880
Fax: 866-398-2908
www.creative-cookies.com

My Lucky Fortune
1510 Hurley Ct.
Hanover, MD 21076
410-690-4463
www.myluckyfortune.com

Sprouted-Wheat Tortillas

Trader Joe's Co.
Various locations
www.traderjoes.com

music

Amazon.com
800-201-7575 (toll-free)
www.amazon.com

Borders
Various locations
734-477-1100
888-81BOOKS (toll-free)
www.borders.com

iTunes
www.apple.com/itunes

party supplies

Beads, Crafts, Cookie Cutters, Decorations, Flowers

Artbeads.com
11901 137th Ave. Ct. KPN
Gig Harbor, WA 98329
253-857-3433
866-715-BEAD (2323)
   (toll-free)
Fax: 253-857-2385
www.artbeads.com

Asian Ideas, Inc.
457 W Lincoln St.
Easton, PA 18042
877-407-9259 (toll-free)
www.asianideas.com

The Bead Shop
158 University Ave.
Palo Alto, CA 94301
650-383-3408
www.beadshopboutique.com

Beau Coup
201 San Antonio Circle,
   Suite 135
Mountain View, CA 94040
877-988-BEAU (2328)
   (toll-free)
www.beau-coup.com

Bridge Kitchenware Corp.
49 Eagle Rock Ave.
East Hanover, NJ 07936
212-688-4220
www.bridgekitchenware.com

Celebrate Express
11232 120th Ave. NE, Ste 204
Kirkland, WA 98033
800-424-7843 (toll-free)
www.celebrateexpress.com

Cost Plus World Market
Various locations
877-World Market
(967-5362) (toll-free)
www.worldmarket.com

Create For Less
6932 SW Macadam Ave.
   Suite A
Portland, OR 97219
866-333-4463 (toll-free)
www.createforless.com

Flax Art & Design
1699 Market St.
San Francisco, CA 94103
415-552-2355
888-352-9278 (toll-free)
www.flaxart.com

Hanging beaded curtains
Michaels
Various locations
800-642-4235 (toll-free)
www.michaels.com

Oriental Trading Company
800-875-8480 (toll-free)
www.orientaltrading.com

Paper Source
Various locations
888-PAPER-11 (toll-free)
www.paper-source.com

Pearl River
477 Broadway
New York, NY 10013
212-431-4770
800-878-2446 (toll-free)
www.pearlriver.com

Target
Various locations
800-591-3869 (toll-free)
www.target.com

Walmart
Various locations
800-966-6546 (toll-free)
www.walmart.com

Wild Things
928-855-6075
www.shopwildthings.com

Williams-Sonoma
Various locations
877-812-6235 (toll-free)
www.williams-sonoma.com

reference books
An Invitation to Tea
Emilie Barnes
Harvest House Publishers,
   1996
Eugene, OR

The New Tea Book
Sara Perry
Chronicle Books, 2001
San Francisco, CA

The Story of Tea
Mary Lou Heiss and
   Robert J. Heiss
Ten Speed Press, 2007
Berkeley, CA 94707

Steeped In Tea
Diana Rosen
Storey Books, 1999
Pownal, VT

tea
Alice's Tea Cup
102 West 73rd St.
New York, NY 10023
212-734-4TEA (4832)
www.alicesteacupgifts.com

Celestial Seasonings
The Hain Celestial Group, Inc.
4600 Sleepy Time Drive
Boulder, CO 80301
800-351-8175 (toll-free)
www.celestialseasonings.com

Cooks Shop Here
65 King St.
Northampton, MA 01060
866-584-5116 (toll-free)
www.cooksshophere.com

In Pursuit of Tea
33 Brook St.
Cornwall Bridge, CT 06754
866-TRUE TEA
www.inpursuitoftea.com

R.C. Bigelow, Inc.
201 Black Rock Turnpike
Fairfield, CT 06825-5512
888-BIGELOW (244-3569)
   (toll-free)
www.bigelowtea.com

Republic of Tea
The Minister of Supply
P.O. Box 1589
Novato, CA 94948
800-298-4TEA (4832)
www.republicoftea.com

Simpson & Vail
P.O. Box 765
3 Quarry Rd.
Brookfield, CT 06804
800-282-8327 (toll-free)
www.svtea.com

Stash Tea
P.O. Box 910
Portland, OR 97207
503-624-1911
800-826-4218 (toll-free)
www.stashtea.com

Strand Tea Company
P.O. Box 580
Sandy, OR 97055
503-668-5348
888-718-6358 (toll-free)
www.strandtea.com

index

table of equivalents

The exact equivalents in the following tables have been rounded for convenience.

LIQUID/DRY MEASUREMENTS

U.S.	METRIC
¼ teaspoon	1.25 milliliters
½ teaspoon	2.5 milliliters
1 teaspoon	5 milliliters
1 tablespoon (3 teaspoons)	15 milliliters
1 fluid ounce (2 tablespoons)	30 milliliters
¼ cup	60 milliliters
⅓ cup	80 milliliters
½ cup	120 milliliters
1 cup	240 milliliters
1 pint (2 cups)	480 milliliters
1 quart (4 cups, 32 ounces)	960 milliliters
1 gallon (4 quarts)	3.84 liters
1 ounce (by weight)	28 grams
1 pound	448 grams
2.2 pounds	1 kilogram

LENGTHS

U.S.	METRIC
⅛ inch	3 millimeters
¼ inch	6 millimeters
½ inch	12 millimeters
1 inch	2.5 centimeters

OVEN TEMPERATURES

FAHRENHEIT	CELSIUS	GAS
250	120	½
275	140	1
300	150	2
325	160	3
350	180	4
375	190	5
400	200	6
425	220	7
450	230	8
475	240	9
500	260	10